I GREW UP, NOW WHAT?

I Grew Up, Now What?

Val Kerr

Boost Communications, Inc.

I Grew Up, Now What?
Val Kerr

Boost Communications, Inc.
Published by Boost Communications, Inc.
Copyright © 2018 by Val Kerr

All rights reserved.

No part of this publication may be reproduced, distributed, or transmitted in any form or by any means, including photocopying, recording, or other electronic or mechanical methods, without the prior written permission of the publisher, except in the case of brief quotations embodied in critical reviews and certain other noncommercial uses permitted by copyright law. For permission requests, write to the publisher, addressed "Attention: Permissions Coordinator," at the address below.

Boost Communications, Inc.
193 Walnut Street
Montclair, NJ 07042

E-mail: info@boostcomm.com

Limit of Liability/Disclaimer of Warranty:
While the publisher and author have used their best efforts in preparing this book, they make no representations or warranties with respect to the accuracy or completeness of the contents of this book and specifically disclaim any implied warranties of merchantability or fitness for a particular purpose. No warranty may be created or extended by sales representatives or written sales materials. Neither the publisher nor author shall be liable for any loss of profit or any other commercial damages, including but not limited to special, incidental, consequential, or other damages.

Publishing and editorial team:
Author Bridge Media, www.AuthorBridgeMedia.com
Project Manager and Editorial Director: Helen Chang
Editor: Jenny Shipley
Publishing Manager: Laurie Aranda
Publishing Coordinator: Iris Sasing

Library of Congress Control Number: 2018900888

ISBN: 978-0-9998491-0-1 – softcover
978-0-9998491-1-8 – hardcover
978-0-9998491-2-5 -- ebook

Ordering Information:
Quantity sales. Special discounts are available on quantity purchases by corporations, associations, and others. For details, contact the publisher at the address above.

Printed in the United States of America

This book is dedicated to all dreams come true—to all of you who have graced my life and all who will. And especially to my son, Ryan, my greatest wish upon on a star.

Acknowledgments

This journey would not have been possible without the brilliance, magic, and support of so many people.

First and foremost, I want to thank my husband, Rob, who always encourages me to "go for it" regardless of the dream I'm dreaming.

Thank you to my mom and dad who knew to "cut the strings" on my sixteenth birthday and let me fly. You had my back then, and ever since.

Thank you to Katherine MacKenett, Jenny Shipley, Helen Chang, and the entire Author Bridge Media team for bringing this dream to reality. You were the fuel for this fire and the sparkle in the magic.

Finally, I want to thank every one of you who have shared your kindness and light in my world during the difficult times. It is from you I have learned that unicorns do exist. I'm grateful to Mrs. Didden, Gayle, Arni, Max, Lori, Brenda, Mr. Carlucci, Aunt Claire, Stevie B., Kiki, Aunt Joan, Susan, Dr. Todd, Scotty-whatty-du-da-day, and all of you not mentioned—you know who you are.

Contents

Acknowledgments 7
Chapter 1 **Dream in Color** 11
Chapter 2 **What Is a *Real* Unicorn?** 23
Chapter 3 **The Unicorn Mindset** 34
Chapter 4 **Your Magic Spark** 45
Chapter 5 **Just *Fly*** 57
Chapter 6 **Envision Your Magical Life** 67
Chapter 7 **Just *Be*** 79
About the Author 86

Chapter 1

DREAM IN COLOR

Lost Dreams

She sits on the porch contemplating the horizon
little girl dreams lost
pensive and somber
Wondering what happened to her joy,
those years too long
Eyes closed, she sees—*From the day I was born*
If only I lived like a Unicorn

A Cage of Unfulfillment

Trying to fit in and follow all the rules is *exhausting*.

You've learned that the hard way. Some days, you feel like the last straggling rat at the end of the race. Even when you take the path of least resistance and just let things happen, life doesn't feel easy.

Which isn't fair. Because you've done everything you're "supposed" to do.

You wake up in the morning, drag yourself to the kitchen, put on the coffee, and start making breakfast for the family before your eyes are even open. You grab the same piece of toast with the same jelly you have every day and consume it without tasting it.

As you sit in your car, in the same traffic jam, on your way to the same job with the same boring projects, you don't even notice your surroundings. At five o'clock, you leave work and do the whole thing in reverse, this time trying to think of what you can quickly make for dinner. You might even have a few minutes to yourself to watch TV or scroll through social media.

Life has become insipid and colorless.

You know you should be grateful for all you have—a roof over your head, a beautiful family, and a job that helps pay the bills—but underneath it all lurks a constant gnawing sense of unfulfillment.

Because however you "should" feel . . . something is missing.

You're not *happy*. Every now and then, as you zone out with your laptop, you click on a picture or video or song from your past and feel a glimmer of happiness.

In those moments, maybe right before falling asleep, you catch a glimpse of the person you once were.

You remember what it felt like to feel such *joy*. You remember that sense of wonder you had when you were a child, that sense of freedom and endless possibilities.

Is it possible that the child you once were is still inside of you? Is it possible—somehow—to recapture that feeling?

Boundless Possibility

The path back to that joy, freedom, and wonder you felt as a child still exists. You can dig it back up like an archaeologist—no matter how many years of dust and grime have settled over it, hiding it from view. And you can rescue your childhood dreams, no matter how deeply buried they may be. How?

By letting go of the expected life you have been living—and starting to live like a unicorn.

Your inner unicorn is something your younger self embraces with a heart wide open. It is a powerful force that will release you from the prison of your humdrum day-to-day existence and breathe adventure and inspiration into your new, magical life.

Imagine this: You wake up in the morning, and instead of crawling out of bed like a zombie, you *jump* out of bed, energized and grateful to start the new day. You hop in the shower, get dressed, and make coffee, fully engaged in each moment. You marvel over the color of the flowers growing outside your kitchen window as you inhale the sumptuous aroma of the coffee brewing and savor every bite of the fluffy frittata you've made from scratch. Your eyes close, just for a moment, to absorb the peaceful blessing you feel in the warmth of the sun shining into the room.

As you pack lunches, kiss your family good-bye, and drive to work, you have amazing ideas about things that excite you. You can't keep from jotting them down before you start your work day, full of gratitude and appreciation for every moment and every thought that crosses your mind.

And guess what? You actually *like* your job. Either you've found a way to make it more enjoyable, or you've created a new position that makes every day more amazing—using your unicorn magic, of course. It took courage to make it happen, but you now spend each day doing exactly what you've always dreamed of doing—and you're loving every minute of it.

When you come home, you're no longer counting down the hours until you finally get to have your fifteen minutes of "you time." *All* your time is you time now, because spending time with your family is open and joyful. You truly appreciate every moment with them. You *see* the beautiful people your children are becoming. You really *look* at your significant other and value all he or she does for your family.

Your loved ones notice your zest for life and feel accepted for who they are. And before long, they start to respond in kind, seeing you for who *you* really are now too.

When you climb into bed, you no longer pass out cold, craving oblivion. The awful restlessness that gnawed at you before is gone. Instead, you dream about your life. In the very moment when you close your eyes, you feel a sense of peace—one that has evaded you for so many years. Satisfied, you gently drift off to sleep.

You are, finally, fulfilled.

Living life as a unicorn is amazing because it is so *free*. You can break the rules, so you can do and be whatever you want. The cage of boredom and unfulfillment loses its power and evaporates—just like that. Now your life is again one of boundless possibilities, just as it was before you grew up. You've become who you once were—that powerful, inspired, limitless little child—again.

You have found unicorn life.

My Unicorn Life

I have always been a dreamer, so unicorn life came to me early. But like every other unicorn, I didn't find it without a rite of passage.

When I was younger, I was a heavy child. In our home, as in many others, food was provided as a way to show love and, at times, a way to keep us kids quiet. Apparently, I was both noisy and *very* loved. When I was twelve years old, the family physician asked me if I was in a weight contest with my father. I weighed 190 pounds. And I felt horrible. I wasn't comfortable in my own skin.

I can't remember every name I was called, but I remember how stuck I felt in this very miserable place. I often went to school wearing my dad's shirt over my pants, trying to hide the size of my body. I couldn't climb the ropes in gym class because I couldn't lift my own weight.

Sure, it was humiliating sitting out while everyone else climbed the ropes easily, but it was more humiliating to be called names in front of everyone.

Then one day, I had enough.

Another person made yet another fat joke at my expense, and that was it—all the mortification that had built up over the years crashed in on me. That afternoon, I came home from school, locked myself in my room, got down on my knees by my bed, and cried. I begged for help to learn how to change my body into one I could be comfortable in.

In that moment, I decided I didn't want to live like that anymore. I reached in and found a place inside myself that said, "I can do this. I can beat this. I can be better than this. I can be what I want to be."

That night, I read a book called *The Scarsdale Diet* from cover to cover. For the next two months, I followed a modified version of the diet. For exercise, I would dance in my room for one hour every day without fail. My determination was tested every time my family offered me something from my "foods to avoid" list, yet I always turned them down. Some days, I even bought my favorite pie and brought it home to them—just to prove to myself that I was strong enough not to eat it.

My plan worked. By September, I had lost sixty pounds.

I went into eighth grade almost half the size I had been the year before. And physically at least, I felt amazing. That part of me was fulfilled in a way it had never been.

But internally, I knew I wasn't done. *What more can I become?* I wondered.

That summer, I discovered I had the power to change things. That day became the beginning of a lifelong journey toward creating a fulfilling unicorn life, not just for myself, but for others as well.

Undercover Unicorn Instructor

I like to call myself an "undercover unicorn instructor." Even when I am not actively teaching about the unicorn life, I still deliver the message to everyone I work with.

Since the early 1990s, I have been secretly teaching people in top law firms, corporations, and other organizations how to live the unicorn life. I've helped manage their technology, processes, and project teams to achieve the best results, seeding the unicorn life into all of it.

I have shared the message of the unicorn life—directly and covertly—with thousands of people around the country. And those thousands of people have gone on to help thousands more people themselves. Because people who make the leap into living a unicorn life never keep it to themselves. They feel more inspired and have a greater appreciation for their lives. They come alive to their own potential. And they want others to feel that way too.

In 2013, I took a leap of my own—from an undercover instructor to a full-time one.

I loved the impact I made as a consultant, teaching the unicorn life undercover. But I knew that my calling was to help people even more directly. So I founded Boost® Life Coaching and started coaching the unicorn life in the full light of day.

The transition out of the corporate world that I had lived, breathed, and loved for more than two decades took courage. But the results have been greater than I ever imagined. Every time I see the "unicorn light" come on again in someone's eyes, I know I made the right decision.

And now it's your turn.

Your Power Partner

This is our opportunity for me to share with you how to live your own unicorn life.

But understand that this book is not going to do the work for you. It's not going to take your place and allow you to be a passive bystander in your transformation. Rather, it is an equal partner in the process to help you realize your infinite potential.

I am the guide, but I do not have power over your magic tools. You are the authority of *you*. And only you have control of your life.

Within these pages, you will find practical ideas and inspiring stories of other people who have experienced the unicorn transformation. Use these guidelines to take back your own power. Write notes in the margin when you feel moved to do so. Use the partnership you find in this book along with a journal, if you are so inspired, so that you can look back at how far you've come. Document your own journey on the path to fulfillment.

We all have different life experiences—and those are to your advantage when you use them as inspiration for change. When you do, you will be able to reclaim your unicorn life.

Why? Why *Not?*

At this point, you may be asking, "Unicorn magic? Really? Can I *really* do this?"

To that I reply, "Why *wouldn't* you be able to do it?"

You are amazing, with limitless creativity and power already living inside you as your birthright. Why *wouldn't* you be able to do absolutely anything you can dream of for yourself?

This doesn't mean the road ahead will be easy. But even if it feels hard, don't give up. Look at yourself. Look at your notes. Look at where you've come from, and believe in what you can be—*whatever* you want that to be.

That day I fell to my knees and cried in my bedroom was the lowest I've ever felt. But it also marked the beginning of a change for me. Because that was the day I began to believe in my own power to change my life from mediocre to magical.

This book is going to give you the tools to believe in yourself too. If I can do it, you can do it. And the freedom you feel when you embrace life as a unicorn will be worth every step of effort between here and there.

Once you take this message into your heart, you won't even need to question it anymore.

You will truly know, without a doubt, that you can do anything. Just like *that*.

Chapter 2

WHAT IS A *REAL* UNICORN?

My Friend, the Unicorn

Some people start out with the unicorn essence early on and lose their way later in life. Some people never find a way to live like unicorns. But a few magical people never lose that sense of unicorn living they had when they were children.

I have a friend named Max—my own role model, actually—who has been a unicorn his entire life.

Max had a challenging start to life. Nothing was handed to him, and he had to work hard for everything he achieved. When he was young, his dream was to be a pilot, so he spent his early teenage years saving up for flying lessons. Max did achieve pilot status, and that was just the start of his success. He never stopped believing in excellence and reaching higher.

Max never has a negative word to say about anyone or anything. When asked a question, he makes it a point to never say no. When he can't say yes, he responds with a maybe. He leaves options open for every opportunity.

Ultimately, Max became a self-made billionaire, and he helped me see life from a different perspective. I witnessed generosity, kindness, success, and wealth all in one person, which I hadn't believed possible. He reminds me to always dream bigger.

I once asked him, "Max, do you think I can fly one of these jets?"

And without hesitation, he replied, "Yeah, maybe someday!"

From that day forward, I've followed his example: never a no, always a yes or maybe, and with one eye fixed firmly toward the night sky.

What Is a *Real* Unicorn?

Max has been successful his entire life, but that's not what makes him a unicorn. In fact, it is because he started out a real unicorn that he has seen much of that success.

But what is a *real* unicorn anyway? And why should you want to live like one?

Unicorns are people who know without a doubt that they can do anything. They don't take the easy way out, because that's not the way toward growth. Instead, unicorns get really clear on what they want to achieve—and then take action to do it.

And unicorns are free. They don't have self-imposed rules or thoughts of "I can't do this." Unicorns have confidence. They are active participants in society, but they don't let societal norms rule them. Unicorns chart the course of their own magical lives.

You can live like a unicorn too.

When you embrace a unicorn life, success becomes action on your own terms. You can be actively involved in charting your course and making decisions about your own life. If you are currently struggling in some way, you can choose to rise up as a unicorn to overcome your challenges. You have that power and authority in your life.

Some people, though, let fear win. They are too afraid to embrace the unicorn life, so they lose their power. They remain unfulfilled and unremarkable.

That insignificance grows every time they don't do what they wish they could, until they risk being eaten alive by feelings of irrelevance. Ultimately, people who run away from the unicorn life end up losing themselves.

Meanwhile, those with the courage to become unicorns are a force for good.

Unicorns create, not destroy. We lead, not follow. We show up and set new standards. But being a unicorn doesn't mean just doing whatever you want, especially if those things are negative. Instead, the unicorn life is about doing what you want in the service of creativity and positivity—even in the face of fear.

The Hunted Unicorn

It is all too easy to forget our uniqueness and our unicorn lives when we get wrapped up in fear.

Let's take a look at Maslow's hierarchy of human needs (which just so happens to be shaped like a unicorn horn) to see how fear can affect our unicorn lives.

What is a *Real* Unicorn 27

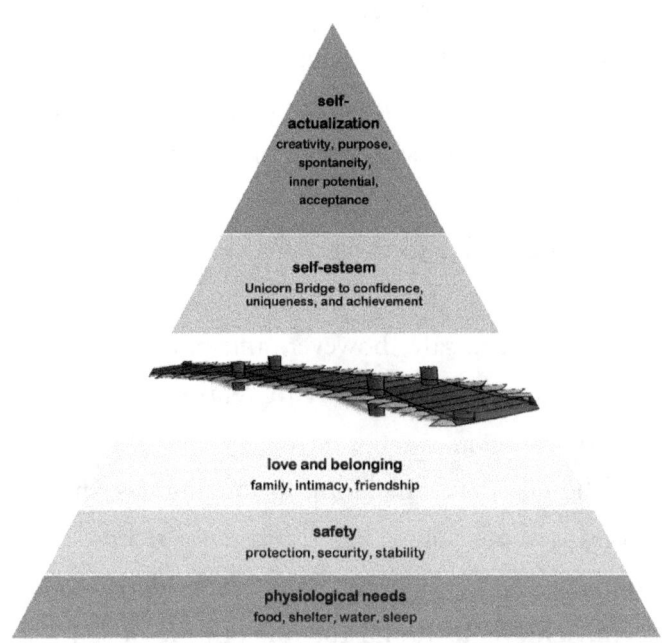

Unicorn Bridge/Maslow Hierarchy

Image Credit: Author

Created by American psychologist Abraham Maslow, the hierarchy has five tiers, the highest of which is self-actualization or fulfillment, and what I am calling the unicorn life.

Maslow says you should achieve each fundamental level before you can move on to the next. With the exception of the first level, I propose that many of the levels can work simultaneously.

The bottom, most basic levels are safety and survival. If we don't have a sense of safety every day, we will feel hunted. And if we are all fraught with fear, we will be unable to thrive. We will simply be trying to survive.

Once we're safe, however, and our physiological needs are met, we can start to venture into unicorn territory.

The next level, including belongingness and love needs, is about your relationships and friends, which contribute to a richer life. This is the bridge to self-esteem, achievement, and the unicorn life of self-actualization, understanding your purpose, and reaching your full potential. This is the ultimate realization where inspiration and joy is seeded.

This is where the unicorn lives.

Rescue Your Childhood Dreams

One of the biggest things that keeps us frozen in place and prevents us from catapulting into a unicorn life is the concept of social norms.

Preconceptions about your role in society may be holding you back from becoming a unicorn. Rather than going after our real potential, we may hold back and accept a role just to fit in or because it is the path of least resistance.

As children, we were often asked, "What do you want to be when you grow up?" What were your childhood dreams? To be a doctor? An astronaut? The president? And then what happened? If you are like most people, you let life happen to you instead of creating and charting your own course.

Some people get trapped by time. We have only so many hours in a day, and you may be exhausted after going through the motions. Others are trapped by finances. And some are trapped by their own state of mind. They tell themselves, "I can't follow that dream; I am too old" or some other limiting statement.

Fear of judgment and criticism makes us take roles that have nothing to do with our childhood dreams. I'm not saying you can't be fulfilled in these roles, but when you feel trapped and they keep you down rather than lift you up, they cross a line.

When we abide by social norms, influenced by how our peers think we should act, we lose our uniqueness. Our potential and authentic selves are squashed as we jockey to fit in. And we are taught that this is the only acceptable way to be a grown-up.

Growing up comes with the expectation that you are automatically supposed to take care of everybody else ahead of yourself. When we put everybody else first, however, we forget about ourselves. We are at the bottom of our own lists. Living for everyone else—running around to meet their goals and going through the motions—means giving up our essence.

Not growing up means being a unicorn. And that means you're not going to be defined by those roles. You are going to live beyond them.

The Road to the Unicorn Life

In the rest of this book, you are going to learn how to break the rules, defy the boxes society wants to shove you into, and rediscover your inner unicorn.

You were born a unicorn. You came into the world with a natural sense of joy, excitement, and wonder about who you are and what you can do. The next five chapters will help you recapture that sense of wonder as you travel down the road to your own unicorn life, from changing your mindset to becoming a *real* unicorn at last.

> ***The unicorn mindset.*** Your unicorn mindset is a new way of looking at the world and at your life—like you did when you were a little child. When you release your fear, you take back control of your power center. This is the first key to unlocking personal fulfillment, because this mindset shift shows you that you are a person who is worthy of happiness in your own life.
>
> ***Your magic spark.*** Your magic spark lies deep within your heart center. When you reconnect with your intuition as a guiding light, you get back in touch with the original joy you had as a child. You will know without a doubt what you want to do, and you will invent ways to make it happen. Finding your magic spark will help you start to

feel alive again as that sparkle of joy returns to you.

Just fly. Unless you let your magic spark grow, it will fizzle. When you take action, you nurture that little spark into a warm, crackling fire. Releasing the need for perfection and working through your challenges help you learn the steps to accomplish your unicorn-life goals.

Envision your magical life. Envisioning your magical life is about visualizing the future that you want—not just letting things happen to you. Creating a plan—a vision for your life—will give you a sense of freedom that will allow you to bring your own dreams to life.

Just be. Once you are living your unicorn life, take a step back to look at your accomplishments, appreciate how far you've come, and recognize where you are in the process. Then stay open to even more unexpected possibilities. Being grateful is the ultimate enricher of your unicorn life.

As you can see, only five steps stand between you and your unicorn life.

Before you move through the rest of this book along the road to rediscovering your inner unicorn, take note of exactly how you feel right now. Are you afraid? Excited? Are you ready to believe in yourself?

When you're ready, get set, because it's time to fly—into the unicorn mindset.

Chapter 3

THE UNICORN MINDSET

Time Flies

About a year after my husband and I had our son, I went to get my nails done.

I hadn't had a manicure in ages—though I used to get them every week—and it was something I wanted to do for myself.

My husband was home, so I knew my son was taken care of. I chose a beautiful color. And I settled into the massage chair to soak my poor, tired cuticles.

I closed my eyes, but my son's face swam into view. I nudged it away. Then my vision swirled with thoughts of everything I had to do at home: the dishes in the sink, the unmade beds, the unvacuumed floors. I opened one eye to peek at the clock. How long is this going to take? I wondered. And why couldn't the nail technician file faster?

The appointment was for one and a half hours, and I needed to get back home. I had a baby to take care of!

But did I, really? Couldn't I be away from the house, my son—from other people's needs and wants—for two hours?

About halfway through my manicure, I finally realized I had to turn off the voices that were competing for my attention. I'm not a criminal here, I told myself. I deserve to have part of my day, just for me, to do what I want to do without feeling guilty about it.

When I got home, no tragedy had befallen anyone, in spite of my husband's "Where are you?" texts. I was refreshed, happier, and reenergized to be with my family.

Now when I get my nails done, I'm able to fully relax for the entire appointment. And the only thought in my head is, "Wow, that feels good."

The Unicorn Mindset

When I dealt with the voices in my mind that were standing in my way, I put myself in the right mental position to become a unicorn.

I put myself in the unicorn mindset.

The ultimate goal of living the unicorn life is to achieve the top two tiers of Maslow's hierarchy (from chapter 2). That means building esteem—both your own self-esteem, which contributes to your own goals and happiness, and that of others.

The unicorn life is also about living more creatively, more spontaneously, and without prejudice. To do so, we need a unicorn mindset, which is about being more joyful. And joy can't be contained. It's always contagious. It illuminates outward and grows from there.

Without the right mindset, it is very difficult—if not impossible—to achieve the unicorn life. Someone who is not positive and who doesn't expect good things won't ever achieve it. When you are positive, however, and you take on the unicorn mindset, you will find that it is the door between your current life and your new, magical life.

The unicorn mindset, like the esteem tier of Maslow's hierarchy, is the bridge you need to build before anything else can happen in your unicorn life.

This chapter shows you how to overcome fear, find your unicorn mindset by redefining selfishness, and push back against pushback.

Amygdala Is Not a *Star Wars* Character

The first task in creating your unicorn mindset is outsmarting your amygdala.

The amygdala is an almond-shaped set of neurons in the limbic system of our brain where fear lives. It is responsible for detecting and responding to threats. And as we discussed in the last chapter, when we go about our day in fear, we can't reach those higher pillars of Maslow's hierarchy. People who are living in fear are unable to cross the bridge into unicorn life. They are stuck.

The amygdala drives our fears. But there's a catch.

It drives our actions as well.

That's why, if you can just get control of it, your amygdala becomes your power center as a unicorn.

Fear isn't always a bad thing, of course. Your amygdala controls your fight-or-flight reaction. It was useful when we were cave dwellers, so if a saber-toothed tiger was coming up behind us, we would run instead of standing around to be eaten alive. In cases like that, a little fear is a useful thing to have!

What we have to do, however, is understand what constitutes a true fear—like walking through a lion's den, terrified of being mauled—and which fears are self-imposed due to a buildup of our own perceptions. This can be a fear of public speaking or of going to the dentist. It can be a fear of failing, of not being accepted, or even a fear of dying.

The biggest fear that holds us back from becoming a unicorn is the fear of not being good enough. When you give in to these fears, you trap yourself with your own mindset.

To live a strong unicorn life, we must overcome our self-imposed fear. And a big part of that is wrenching ourselves free of what other people think of us. Much of the time, that begins with redefining selfishness.

Redefining Selfish

The first step in taking back your control and overcoming your fears is to ask yourself, "If you are afraid of not being good enough, whose expectations are you living up to?"

If the answer is everybody's but your own—your parents', your friends', your spouse's, or even society's expectations—then you know where you got those expectations in the first place: roles and boxes that you no longer want to force yourself into.

So the first thing to do to develop a unicorn mindset is to stop worrying about what others think about you—especially if the world has taken to calling you selfish every time you try to practice a little self-care (my manicure, for instance).

Easy to say, right? But it can be very difficult to implement.

First, I want to be clear that I am not saying you shouldn't give of yourself to other people. Instead, you must include yourself among the people you're giving to.

We often become the forgotten people in our own lives. And you don't want to feel that way anymore. You don't want to be a doormat. But at the same time, if you take some time for yourself, you feel selfish. Right?

Well, when you feel unacknowledged and invisible in your own life, it is time to redefine the word "selfish."

The dictionary definition of selfish is "having or showing concern only for yourself and not for the needs or feelings of other people." The key word there is "only." When people think of *only* themselves, they are selfish.

But taking time for yourself for self-care is not selfish. So how do we know where to draw the line?

When we're in balance, we can feel when we cross the line and push ourselves too far, and we can sense what we need in order to keep ourselves healthy and happy. If you have been putting others first and yourself last for a long time, you most likely have not yet achieved that balance.

So here is a benchmark to go by: until you are doing enough for yourself to feel a sense of wholeness, you have not crossed the line into selfishness. Once you know you are doing enough—when you feel whole again—then you will be in balance. And that benefits everybody around you as well. It seems counterintuitive, but when you show up as your most authentic self, it will make the people around you happier.

Remember: joy is contagious! And that's the kind of outbreak a unicorn loves to catch.

Pushing Back

But what if you experience some pushback as you begin to shift into your unicorn mindset?

Your loved ones are used to you always being available to fill their needs. Now you're starting to make a change, to make your needs as important as everyone else's. You may already be dealing with guilt, and that can increase if you don't get the support you need when making this change.

As hard as it may be, you can't let the pushback be an excuse to let yourself off the hook. You must learn to communicate openly about your needs.

Once you've realized that you need to make a change, sit down and have an open talk with your family and friends. Be honest with them about your recent mindset shift, and explain why this change is so necessary. When you do, speak from a place of compassion and strength. Remember that your loved ones are going to see you making changes and feeling great about it, and they may feel inadequate or afraid of being left behind. Their amygdalae may be sending them fear signals, because change is scary.

Reassure them, but be very clear in your own mind. You need to be whole, and you can't be your best and start living your unicorn life until that happens.

The changes you are making are not *against* your family; they're *for* you. The final mindset piece that needs to change is the thinking that if you're doing something for yourself, then you must be taking something away from your loved ones. The reality is this: as your unicorn mindset grows stronger, you will be able to remain whole within yourself and give them more than ever.

Mindset Maintenance

The work doesn't end once you have found your unicorn mindset. You have to maintain your new mindset like a garden, watering and nurturing it diligently every day.

One way of doing that is to have a morning ritual that you engage in every day. A great way to wake up is to recite incantations to put you in a state of positivity and strength.

I like to recite to myself, "Now, I am the voice. I will lead, not follow. I will believe, not doubt. I will create, not destroy. I am a force for good. I will set a new standard and step up, step up, step up!" That is my unicorn mantra, which is adapted from motivational author Tony Robbins.

Other phrases that I say three times daily are "I am a healing machine" and "My cells flow with love, health, and vitality."

It is important to find incantations that resonate within you. Feel free to use mine, or choose words and phrases you can relate to. When you find the right words, don't just mumble them under your breath. You must stand tall and say them out loud and with passion to make the magic work!

Every time you do, you'll be nurturing the unicorn mindset you have discovered so that it can always keep growing.

The Cornerstone of Unicorn Life

Your unicorn mindset is the cornerstone, the heart of everything you are going to learn, for your new, magical life. And the stronger your mindset is, the more easily you will be able to take all the other parts of it and unify them.

In chapter 2, we discussed the esteem bridge that you cross on the way to a self-actualized unicorn life. With your unicorn mindset in place, you are ready to leap across that first level of Maslow's pyramid and into your unicorn life.

But just as you must walk before you can run, you must learn to be light before you can take your flying leap as a unicorn. Chapter 4 will show you how to dig deep to find the light of your magic spark.

Chapter 4

YOUR MAGIC SPARK

The Wonder of Washing Dishes

Every Thanksgiving, my sister and I loved doing the dishes together.

Most people probably think of a huge pile of dirty pots and plates as pure drudgery. But for us, it was a time to reconnect. Those talks at the kitchen sink were the highlight of the year for us—something we both looked forward to in our separate lives.

When everyone was done eating, we would go around the table and collect all the plates, glasses, and silverware. We often had twenty people for Thanksgiving dinner, so there were tons of dishes afterward. And we usually used the good china, so they all had to be hand washed.

It would take us hours to get everything done, but we didn't even notice.

I washed each dish and handed it to her to dry and put away. She liked that part best, so it was perfect. And as we reminisced and laughed, something magical happened.

The rest of the family gravitated toward the kitchen. They settled in around us, just to listen in as we had fun.

And the kitchen sink—possibly the least exciting place you can imagine—was transformed into a gathering place of love and joy.

Your Magic Spark

When we did the dishes, my sister and I weren't setting out to entertain people and make them happy; we were getting in touch with our magic sparks.

Your magic spark is your brightness. It is a feeling that comes when you are full of life. You felt it when you were little, running through the sprinklers and jumping in puddles. It is the notion that you can do anything and be anybody you want to be. And it can infuse your whole life with wonder.

We tend to forget our magic sparks when we grow up, as we become teenagers and have all those hormones coursing through our systems. We put more emphasis on what other people think of us. We learn how they want us to act. We take on new roles, following along, even if they don't quite fit. But unless we find a way to rescue our childhood dreams and rediscover our unique magic spark, we will wilt. We will lose our way and never finish walking the path back to our unicorn life.

With your magic spark, however, anything you want to do becomes possible. There is *nothing* you can't do.

When you reclaim your spark, you live life authentically. Your confidence grows, your courage takes over, and you become more joyful. As a result of being joyful, you attract more joy. And ultimately, once you infuse your magic spark into everything in your life—even the most ordinary, everyday tasks, like doing dishes—you become the unicorn you were always born to be.

You were born with a magic spark, so you *can* get it back. It is still there, inside of you. You don't have to create it; you just have to rediscover it.

And you can do that by growing back down, feeding the spark within, and nurturing that spark once you've found it.

Grow Back Down

Part of rediscovering your magic spark is getting in touch with your younger self. You can do that by choosing not to grow up and, instead, grow back down.

Growing up is fraught with the norms, ills, and things we're supposed to do every day. We aren't born with these ideas; we are conditioned by society to receive them. When we are born and as little children, we're happy: we dance when we want to dance, we sing and scream and laugh.

Laughing, incidentally, is a big part of getting back to that child you once were.

One study showed that, on average, children laugh three hundred times per day. By the time we reach adulthood, however, we are much less likely to laugh: only an average of fifteen times per day.

So what makes you laugh?

Maybe you like to go to comedy shows. Maybe you like funny movies or books or comics. Find the things that make you laugh, and engage in more of those.

My dad was awesome about taking videos of me, my siblings, and our cousins when we were younger. I sat down to watch one of those videos the other day, and it was about thirty minutes of me playing and laughing and being silly. All I could think was, "Ah! I was so happy!"

If you think back to when you were a child, you can reunite with those things you loved to do. Maybe you loved coloring or gardening or making pancakes. Whatever it was back then, check your own history for ideas that might help you rescue that inner child again.

And once you rediscover your magic spark, give it the fuel it needs to burn brightly as it guides you toward living like a unicorn.

Feed the Spark

Life is full of distractions. We distract ourselves with so many things all the time. And when we are mindlessly involved in these day-to-day tasks, we prevent ourselves from being in touch with our magic sparks.

Even the things we *have* to do in life can be done more joyfully. When you feed your magic spark, you can find joy in anything—yes, even doing the dishes after Thanksgiving dinner! And even though you're busy and have all these things to do, you can find within them some beautiful moments of settling into yourself. Of stillness. Of being present.

Feeding your magic spark is done by taking a step back, looking at everything as a whole, putting pen to paper, getting in touch with nature, meditating, and moving your body.

Take a step back. The very first thing you want to do is to take a step back. You've been absorbed by distractions for a long time, which led to losing your spark.

Before you can begin settling into yourself, you need to breathe. Rediscovering a lost part of yourself sounds scary, but what is it just to take a breath?

Take stock. Step out of your life for a little while. Take a few hours somewhere you feel blissful, and gradually get to a place where you can see what is working and what isn't.

When you really relax, you are able to take an honest step back and reflect on everything happening in your life. You are now free to begin breaking through all the things that have been holding you back.

Look at everything as a whole. After you have had a chance to take a breath, take a look at your whole situation. What's going on in the present? What has happened in the past that you need to let go of? What do you envision for your future?

Get clear on what you want to do. As you do, let your imagination out of the box it has been trapped in all these years. You don't have to do everything you think of. Just give yourself permission to dream again.

Put it down on paper. Once you are clear, write it down. Make lists of what you want to do. Make lists of things that used to make you laugh. List what you imagined when you played dress-up when you were little.

I used to play dress-up all the time with my siblings and cousins. One time, I played hairdresser and cut my sister's hair for her. That didn't go over too well!

The point is that when we were kids, we would pretend. We'd play make-believe. We'd dream of what we could be. And the adult version of make-believe is to make those lists and start to imagine again.

The best part is that now you can create the things you imagine in a way you couldn't when you were a child.

Write down everything without filtering. You may even want to keep a dream journal or a notebook where you can write down all your inspirational thoughts and ideas.

Try to do this every day. Many people like to do this first thing in the morning, which allows you to write down the things that your dreams reveal.

Writing it down also gives you a record to reflect on as you journey to your unicorn life.

Get in touch with nature. The next part of feeding your magical spark is getting in touch with nature.

You can find nature anywhere—even if you live in a city. You might choose to find your local park and have lunch there. You might be able to find a rooftop garden or create your own natural space outdoors with stones or a waterfall. Or you might even decide to escape to a national park or to the beach.

I love mountains, so I went on a retreat to Sedona, Arizona, to recapture my magic spark. I spent a couple of days there, just getting in touch with nature as a guide to reawaken myself. I live in New York, and sometimes I get lost in all this city metal!

When I hiked in the mountains, things really started to unfold. My mind settled, so I could open it to what was true and what needed to happen next. In nature, things become very clear, open, and endless. This is where you will find the expansiveness of yourself as well as a sense of the earth and of being grounded.

Meditate. Meditation also feeds our magic spark, because it helps us become more mindful. We must go within ourselves to settle internally first, bringing balance back to our lives.

Try to make meditation a daily practice in your life. Every morning, do your best to get up and meditate—even if it's just for five or ten minutes. Start slowly and build up to whatever is comfortable for you. End your day with meditation to reflect on the things you are grateful for in your life.

Daily meditation is your visitation time with the magic spark that lives inside of you.

Move your body. Exercise is one of the best medicines. It feeds your magic spark, whether you run or swim or practice yoga—anything that helps you feel grounded and allows you to subtly settle into yourself. With meditation, your mind settles. With movement, your body can settle too.

For me, I use yoga and running as healthy rituals to get into that state of openness.

I started running when I was twenty-seven, after I traveled to Colorado to watch my cousin run a race.

Huge crowds were all around. As she ran across the finish line, I felt the excitement myself. It inspired me. I said, "I'm going to do that!"

When I got home, I took up running. It built up my discipline as well as my confidence. And it became a significant part of my life. If I didn't run, I felt off that day. Ultimately, running became my daily moving meditation—combining exercise, nature, and meditation in one!

Nurture Your Magic Spark

Now that you have found and fed your magic spark, you will want to nurture it to keep it glowing.

Build a ritual that includes any or all of the things we just talked about. Try to find the joy in everyday things. Initially, it may feel uncomfortable, but as you become more aware and more joyful, it will get easier.

You may have to challenge yourself at first to find something fun or enjoyable about doing the dishes, for example. But then you'll start to notice seemingly insignificant things such as rainbow-colored bubbles that rise from the sink as you wash the last dish. Eventually, you won't have to challenge yourself anymore; you will notice the joy naturally.

Finally, don't be afraid to say yes to life.

When I saw my cousin running and was inspired to start running for fun myself, I could have said, "I don't have time for that. I have all this other stuff I should be doing."

But I didn't. I accepted the invitation I saw before me.

Once you start to do all these things—meditating, moving your body, and getting in touch with nature—you will see yourself becoming more mindful and present. You will find yourself more open to and accepting of new opportunities. When the opportunities come, however, you still have to say yes—and that will grow your magic spark until you feel the joy in every day.

The Excavation

Rediscovering your magic spark might start small. You can begin to add it into your life right away, in things like doing the dishes. Soon, you will begin to find the little things that you enjoy doing naturally.

And then you can start to rescue the bigger dreams that you had when you were a child but buried a long time ago. You're going to pursue them as part of a longer journey—and you will have your magic spark to fuel you all the way.

Now that your dreams are rising again, it's time to pursue them properly. Dreams can't really come true unless they are followed by action. In chapter 5, you are going to learn to move like a unicorn, and just *fly*.

Chapter 5

JUST *FLY*

The Big Bad City

I grew up in the suburbs about thirty miles outside of New York City. My father was a police sergeant, and my mother worried a lot about her children, so I heard all the terrifying stories of the Big Bad City. Only bad things could happen there.

When I was twenty-six, I needed to jump-start my life. I was looking for an accounting job, and one of my friends recommended that I look in New York, where the market was better.

My immediate response was, "I can't go to the city; there are murderers!"

Despite the whispers of danger lurking in the city, I applied for a job and was offered the position, but the company required I start right away. For days to follow, all I could think was, "I can't do it." I declined the offer.

After additional thought and much regret, and despite the dangers and fear, I changed my mind. I called the staffing agency and said, "I *have* to do this!"

On my first day, I was so nervous as I took the bus for my hour-and-a-half commute into the city. I had never been on anything but a school bus before! Then I had to take a subway to the office. It felt like there were a million people all rushing and pushing; it was so hectic.

But it was exciting, too, like the first day of school. Everything was new. I had a new office and a new desk. I was new as well: at that point, I had never had a corporate job. At the end of that first day, I was amazed to realize I hadn't been murdered.

And better still: I was finding my way again.

Just *Fly*

The day I decided to take action—to take that job and go to New York City, in spite of everything I'd heard—was the day I first flew like a unicorn.

Flying like a unicorn means you move forward through your life with the knowledge of what needs to be done. You feel the strength of your commitment, and you have the courage to achieve your goals. Before long, if you practice it often, that feeling of absolute freedom begins to feel natural.

Becoming a unicorn is all about achieving our dreams. In the previous chapter, you found your magic spark and rescued your childhood dreams. But even though you have them, you won't be able to achieve them unless you act. Without taking action and learning to fly like a unicorn as part of the journey toward a magical life, we remain stuck. If we never take action, we never grow—and then our dreams die, withered and lost, without our ever realizing what could have been.

Your dreams have latent potential, and when you take action, those dreams are activated and become real. Whatever you focus on comes true. Then you can experience all the benefits and joy of living as a unicorn.

In just three steps, you can start flying toward your dreams. Those steps are to let go of perfection, tap into your courage, and hold yourself accountable by getting a journal and finding a mentor.

Let Go of Perfection

One of the reasons many people never take action and start to fly like a unicorn is because they are frozen with fear—sometimes fear of success, but more often the fear of failure.

Trying to be perfect is a way of protecting yourself from that fear. Think about it: if you try to do everything perfectly, then you can't fail. What actually happens is that we become too afraid and we never move. We become paralyzed by perfectionism.

So the first step to taking action is to overcome this desperate need to be perfect.

To do so, you must tell yourself that you are okay, whether a result is perfect or not. You are loved, no matter what. We seek to be perfect for acceptance and acknowledgment from our parents, from our teachers, and even at work. We want to know that if we do everything perfectly, we will be seen. We will be loved.

The counterbalance to the need for perfection is to feed your own self-acceptance.

When you give yourself that acceptance, first by adjusting your mindset and then by rediscovering your magic spark, you learn that you don't need external acknowledgment anymore. Now it comes from within. And that deactivates the need for perfection.

From there, you can give yourself permission to fail. Not only that, you can even celebrate your failures. If you've always said your whole life, "I won't do it unless I do it perfectly," then now is the time to *intentionally* do it imperfectly. Color outside the lines. Bake a cake without a recipe and, even if it ends up a messy flop, at least you will have had the experience of trying. Failure has value, just like success does.

Nothing is perfect, and if you're not failing, then you're not learning. Nobody likes to fail, but learning from your failures is what helps you grow. When you become comfortable with failure, you start collecting the experiences that allow you to fly.

Tap Into Your Courage

Once you're okay with messing up, the second piece of learning to fly like a unicorn is to tap into your courage in order to act.

Courage is our inner strength that tells us we can do this, no matter what. Without trusting in our courage—trusting that we can do this and be okay, even in the face of fear—we will become immobilized.

Courage is often glorified and made glamorous. We tend to think of courageous people as valiant, fearless warriors on battlefields with shiny swords and shields. In real life, however, courage may not be shiny or glamorous at all, even though it is incredibly powerful. When it comes down to it, courage is feeling the fear of an action—and doing it anyway.

I have a friend who skydives and goes scuba diving with sharks. He doesn't fear that at all, so it doesn't take much courage for him to do it. I'm afraid of both of those things, and I'm not doing either one. That doesn't bother me, because skydiving and sharks don't make an appearance in my dreams.

On the other hand, I'm also afraid of speaking in front of large audiences—yet I am fulfilled by sharing my message. In this case, my dreams are at stake. So I lead with courage to do it.

For example, when I had to give my master's presentation in front of an audience of fellow Columbia University students, professors, executives, and our sponsors from NASA headquarters, I was truly fearful. I mean, I was *full* of fear.

I was speaking second, so I had plenty of time to build up an unhealthy level of dread. And it seemed like my partner's part of the talk was going on forever. When I stepped up to the microphone, I wasn't sure I would even be able to open my mouth and force the words out.

And then, without thinking about it, I opened with a joke. It just flowed naturally, with perfect timing. Everybody laughed, and I forgot about my fears and kept talking.

And then it was exhilarating.

That act of courage—stepping up to the microphone and making that joke—transformed my fear into confidence and empowerment. Now I'll talk to anyone—any group of people—any time!

The value of courage lies in things you truly believe in—the things you want to achieve but are afraid to do. Unicorns know that you can be afraid and still push through to do it anyway. The payoff is moving ever closer toward your dreams.

And before you know it, your dreams have become realities.

Hold Yourself Accountable

The last piece of taking action is to hold yourself accountable, to keep momentum going. I find the best ways to do that are to get a journal and find a mentor.

Get a journal. In chapter 4, I told you that one of the steps to feeding your magic spark is to put pen to paper. That holds true even after your spark has become a flame and you are burning to take action. Writing it down is still the best way to self-accountability.

Write down all the actions you need to take to live your unicorn life, and then prioritize them. You can do only so many things in a day, so pick the highest-priority things to do now. Then add the rest to your long-term goals.

Make sure that at the top of your list is to practice self-care every day. That written record will show you if you have fallen off track a little bit, so you can easily course correct without losing your spark again.

I like to use a Franklin Covey journal, because they are beautiful and have a great way of keeping you organized. Put stickers all throughout it, if that's what speaks to you. You want your journal to inspire you so that you will pick it up every day.

Find a coach. Once you are holding yourself accountable, you will also want to get different perspectives on ways to achieve your goals. You can do this by working with a coach, someone who has the experience you want and who can help you achieve the success you value. Ideally, your coach should have an attitude you can learn from.

If you'd rather not work with a coach, think of people in your life whom you look up to and who can serve as role models and mentors. You can even have different mentors for different goals. Draw from them the qualities you want to possess in yourself. They don't even have to know they are your role model. You can watch and learn just by paying attention, without ever sitting down and talking in person.

Ideally, though, your mentor is someone who can serve as a life coach. He or she can keep you accountable, too, especially when you are at risk of losing yourself to some of your responsibilities. You have already learned that if something has to fall off the edge and be sacrificed, you are always the first to go.

Your coach can keep you on target, keep you focused, and keep you accountable to yourself, your dreams, and your magic spark.

Unicorns *Can* Fly

Some people will tell you that unicorns can't fly. "You're thinking of a Pegasus," they say.

To them, I reply, "Show me a unicorn that *can't* fly."

And those people can't do it, because unicorns are mythological creatures—and that means they can be anything you want them to be. Unicorns can do anything you believe they can. If you believe it, unicorns can fly.

And so can you.

You have learned to fly, but you have another important step before you are living your best unicorn life. You must learn what that life looks like. In chapter 6, you will learn to envision your magical life.

Chapter 6

ENVISION YOUR MAGICAL LIFE

Jumping into Adventure

My work has always been incredibly important to me. By the age of nineteen, I was regularly working two to three jobs. It wasn't about the money; it was about contributing and learning and being more than I was. I wanted significance. I wanted to contribute in some way. I wanted to change lives.

And that started with my own.

After working at a law firm for ten years—a job that I loved and worked extremely hard at—I had the opportunity to step into a new position at an interactive media company.

The company was brand new. It didn't have any real history—or any revenue—and it required a pay cut. I would be giving up a safe, dependable, familiar position and taking a leap of faith into the unknown. It took a while to convince myself to take that leap.

In the end, it was the excitement for a new opportunity—a bigger future—that decided things for me. I leaped.

And it was an amazing experience. I met incredible people whom I am still friends with today. It was exciting working in a fast-paced world where learning happened rapidly. I was able to travel to London, Amsterdam, and Paris to visit our international offices. Within the first year, not only was I making more money than I had been at my last job, I was finally able to buy my own house—the ultimate feeling of freedom and independence—which I had been dreaming of for years.

That jump into a new adventure brought me one step closer to living my dream life. And it began when my vision of what was possible outweighed the security of where I had already been.

Your Magical Life

You have shifted your mindset and changed the way you look at things. You have found your magic spark, which has given you back your power and your joy. And you are starting to take action toward living your unicorn life.

Now it's time to apply your power and begin envisioning your greatest possible magical life—the future that you want.

Visualizing your new life means that you continue to dream, and now you plan for those dreams. Once that happens, you are living by design instead of by default. And visualization is a critical part of living by design.

We must envision our magical lives before we can build them and live them. As I've said before, what we focus on becomes true. If we don't envision what we want in our lives, then we have no notion of how to set the plan in motion. But when we do envision how we want our futures to look, we can put our plans into action—and make magic happen!

To envision your magical future, you must make a plan, create a vision, and, finally, maintain your vision as you work toward success.

The Design Phase

Before your dreams become realities, you are in the design phase of creating your unicorn life. And that means you have to make a plan to build your own vision.

First, decide which dream you want to focus on initially. This will give you an idea of the basic vision to start with. Then, determine the end goal. What are you trying to achieve by putting this dream in motion? Finally, break the end goal down into steps so you know what resources you need to realize your dream.

I have found that one of the strongest ways to build a vision is to create a vision board. A vision board is a powerful way to keep a visual reminder of your dreams in front of you.

I first created a vision board when I was about thirty years old. At that point, I was just beginning to see what success could look like for me—the freedom and opportunity to have happy times. I had always been a high achiever, but now I had a new job running a department at a law firm. I wanted to be an effective leader, so I had to learn what inspired others.

And I knew I needed to grow myself. Creating this vision board became a beacon for me to grow toward.

Putting my vision board together was a creative process that took a few weeks. I would focus on things that kept coming up in my dreams, things that were important to me. I went through pictures and jotted down memories, and I began to see how they could be realized in the future.

The first vision board I created for inspiration and motivation

My original vision board has a picture from a trip to Aspen, where my mentor, Max, invited me and my family to stay in a gorgeous chalet. The picture is of my mother sitting on the sofa with her celebrity sunglasses on. I included it because she found so much joy in that experience. It was something she had never done before, and it touched her life in a special way. The experience gave me so much inspiration, because I was so excited to be able to give her that opportunity and so happy to see her joy.

I feel a lot of inspiration from running, because it makes me feel my best and gives me energy. So that was also a concept on my vision board. I had a picture of a dream house and a new car. I included cut-out images of a university, along with quotes such as "Just Do It" and many others I found along the way. They became my mantras to live by.

I also included some old pictures on my board—ones that reminded me of times when I felt accomplished. I have a picture of me sitting at my desk at my first job in New York City. It reminds me of what I've achieved, so I can continue the momentum and dream more. I added reminders of family and memories that inspired me. And I included a baby at the very top of my board.

Having those images as inspiration, in front of me every day, has helped me to become a strong leader, one who can help others to see there are no limits to what they can do.

The department I was leading when I created my first vision board doubled in size by the time I left. I ran marathons. I went back to school nights and weekends, finishing an associate's degree, bachelor's degree, and, finally, a graduate degree. And the greatest piece of my vision board came true only when the time was right—the arrival of our baby boy.

By focusing on the positive things I wanted for my future, my vision board opened up my life to the expansiveness of unicorn living.

How to Create Your Own Vision Board

You, too, can create your own vision board to expand the magical future you want for your unicorn life.

There are no set guidelines to follow as you create a vision board. Just get creative, and lose the filter.

Anything goes. Don't give it too much thought initially. Just get in touch with those things that inspire you to be better and the things you dream about. No matter how silly it may seem, just *dream*.

Look through your favorite magazines and snip out pictures, articles, or quotes that speak to your dreams. Use your own drawings or writings if you can't find exactly what you want. You can find images online, but if you create your vision board digitally, be sure to find a way to get it physically into your space. You need to see it every day.

Your vision board can be as big or as small as you want. The essential part is that when you look at it, your vision board inspires you. This is your handy reference as you are building your dreams and taking action toward making them come true.

Even if you're not entirely sure what all the parts of your big, long-term life vision may look like right now, they will start to emerge naturally when you allow yourself to dream.

And once you have your vision board, you can take that vision and make it into a mission.

This is the action step, where you start to break a dream into pieces and actively work toward making it come true.

You will also want to allow for some flexibility in *how* your dreams are realized. As you most likely know, dreams do not always transpire exactly as we expect.

I mentioned earlier that I had pictures of a baby on my vision board. And I actively tried to make that dream come true; my husband and I spent years trying to conceive. It didn't happen as expected for us, but I never gave up on my dream of having a baby. Our baby boy waited for us.

So you never want to look back and say, "My dream is dead." It may need to happen in a way you can't control. We do everything in our power to make our dreams happen, but sometimes we need to hand the reins back to the dreams themselves. That is when we learn to understand that everything happens for a reason, and we have to trust in that.

And then, of course, you can always keep dreaming.

Keep Your Vision Growing

After you create your vision board and begin taking action, you will see amazing things happen. And at some point, all of your dreams will come true, in one way or another. You will look up one day and realize, "Wow, I actually achieved a lot of this. This is my life now!"

At that point, I recommend creating a new vision board. Rather than adding on top of your old dreams, give yourself a new space to explore new ones. If you have dreams on your old vision board that haven't been realized, bring them forward in some way.

Most of the dreams on my original vision board have come true. I am amazed, but not surprised, by how visualizing with laser-like focus has facilitated making these dreams a reality.

I am currently working on a new vision board, and I plan to carry over the few remaining dreams still in action. For example, I have pictures with a music theme, as I love to sing and would like to record an album. I am also adding more images from family and friend gatherings because these get-togethers bring me great joy. I want to include pictures of the places I would like to visit, such as Thailand, southern Italy, and Peru. Finally, I am including quotes from the visionaries who continue to inspire me every day.

Your dreams are going to keep growing and changing, and you're going to have new ones. The process for building new visions and creating a new vision board is the same, even as the dreams you portray become different, bigger—and even better.

Losing Control

When I've tried to control how a dream comes true, or when I've fought the process, it always ends up a disaster.

One of my goals on my vision board speaks to health. I had a health challenge that required a small procedure in my doctor's office. I was nervous about having the procedure done, but I psyched myself up for it to happen. By the time my appointment day rolled around, I was actually excited to have it done, because I was taking charge of my health!

Two hours before my appointment, I got a call from the doctor's office asking if I would mind rescheduling, because the doctor was being called away. I was so disappointed and upset, because I was ready for this to happen—and it had to happen *now*.

The office ended up accommodating me, and I went in for the appointment even though I knew it would be rushed. It was so painful! I remember thinking, "Why did I ever push for this to happen?"

To this day, I always regret trying to push the flow in my favor, because I know it always has bad results. The best way to build a vision is with flexibility: work with your dreams, not on them.

Now that you have done the work of rediscovering your inner unicorn, and you have a clear vision of your magical future, it is time to embrace all that life has to offer you. Chapter 7 will take you to that final step, which is to just *be*.

Chapter 7

JUST *BE*

The Freedom to Be *Me*

Who would have known that one of the biggest turning points for me to truly start living my unicorn life would be when I divorced my first husband?

I come from a very traditional family. I wanted to be the perfect wife, even though trying to fit into that role felt like wearing a scratchy wool suit. I was trapped in the notion of doing what I was taught—sticking with it, figuring it out, dealing with it. If I could only be the helpful one, the good wife, the perfect partner long enough, things would change on their own.

I had all these preconceived notions about a knight in shining armor coming to swoop in and save my life. I was ready to ride off into the sunset together.

It wasn't until I was twenty-six years old that I realized it wasn't going to happen. If anyone was going to save me, it was going to be *me*. It was time to get real.

It took until that moment for me to realize that I could also decide what my future was going to be like.

That's when I discovered true freedom.

I started my career doing amazing work in New York City. Then I decided to go back to school, spending the better part of the next twenty-six years in college in some way. Even after earning three degrees, I am researching PhD programs, because receiving and sharing knowledge is a big part of who I am. But most importantly, I learn something new every single day.

I had a dream for how I wanted my life to turn out—and my life today is even better than I could ever have expected. It's more than a great life.

It's a unicorn life.

Enjoy Your Unicorn Life

You have done all the work of rediscovering your inner unicorn. You rescued the dreams you had before you grew up. And you have set a vision for your new, magical life.

What happens now?

Now you do exactly what you did as you started to find your magic spark: you take a step back, a deep breath. You appreciate everything you've accomplished, and reflect with gratitude every day on the opportunities that have come your way. Take it all in.

After all, what was the point of doing all that work to build your unicorn life if you're not going to enjoy it?

We must take this time to enjoy what we've built. Otherwise, we are just in perpetual motion, without ever really reflecting on it. When you take time for reflection, however, you reconnect with your inner compass. This is when you can stop and just *be*.

At the end, you find the beginning. The cycle keeps going and going. The gratitude you feel fuels your magic spark, which in turn fuels new dreams and visions for your future. Once you are living your new dreams, you will become still again to reflect on those dreams, until your imagination propels you back into action.

This is the unicorn life, in perpetuity.

Out of Time

Even after finding my unicorn life, I had moments where I forgot to just enjoy it.

By 2013, it felt like I had been going to school and/or working full time most of my life. I went to college when I could—sometimes just at night and on weekends. I had accomplished so much: starting a new career, then working my way through college to end up with my degrees. It felt awesome.

But once I was done, I had a sense of, "Okay, now what?"

That's when the fear struck. "You're running out of time," I told myself. "Life isn't going to last forever." I had to get serious!

I thought that I should do what I could to reach all my other goals—and I should do it now. So I tried to do everything at once.

While working full time as a consultant, I signed up for yoga teacher training. To keep the momentum going as a recent graduate from Marist College, I also signed up for my master's program at Columbia University—figuring that if I didn't do it now, I would probably never do it. And I launched my wellness coaching practice, the one thing I knew would make the greatest impact and proved to be my true purpose.

But somewhere in the middle of throwing myself into all that action—between finishing a chapter in my nutrition program, finishing a paper for the master's program, being in yoga teacher training classes, and sitting in four-hour tech meetings, with most days going past midnight—I had a realization:

This isn't fulfilling me.

That day, I followed my own advice again. I took a step back so I could finally take a breath. I checked in with myself. And I realized that there *is* still time. Things will show themselves as needed, and it's not the end of the world if I don't do everything at once, all on my own.

And just as I had that realization, as I let everything finish around me, the process started for me and my husband to have our son. And his timing was impeccable.

So I learned to trust in the timing. You don't need to push it. You don't need to try to make things happen from a place of fear of running out of time. There is a time for everything, and it will reveal itself to you when you are aligned with your inner unicorn.

When you trust in your own magical spark, everything unfolds as it should.

Find Your Unicorn Herd

Unicorns do not have to be solitary creatures. You do not have to live your unicorn life without support on the journey.

You took my hand in yours when you started reading this book, and if you still feel a little wobbly on your feet, you don't have to let go yet. I've built a safety net to catch you, even after you turn the last page. We can take the next steps together.

Whether you feel you need a coaching session to guide you to your biggest dreams or a hands-on workshop to learn more about visioning, wellness, and the magic of unicorn life, we can walk your path together.

If you reach out, you will find your unicorn herd here.

Life Rises Up

When you have set the vision of your life in motion, life itself will rise up to surprise you in magical ways that go beyond your hopes and dreams.

Live like the child you were, when there were no filters and everything was possible.

Laugh more. Jump in puddles. Build sandcastles. Don't grow up and become disillusioned. And if you *have* grown up and become disillusioned—then grow back down! Replace disillusionment with the dreams that have always been there.

Grow back into innocent joy and wonder. Stand tall, be brave . . .

Then *fly*.

About the Author

Val Kerr believes in the magic that comes from changing your life. From a young age, she studied nutrition, motivation, and wellness—a path that led her from being on track to weigh as much as her father at age thirteen to losing sixty pounds over the summer before eighth grade. Over the past decade, Kerr has turned her passion for wellness and mindfulness into a mission to share her principles for success with others as the founder of Boost® Life Coaching.

Kerr got her start in corporate life working at Triangle Industries, Inc. in New York City in her mid-twenties. While earning her degrees, she provided consulting services to some of the world's top law, technology, and media firms. Kerr holds a graduate degree from Columbia University, undergraduate degrees from New York University and Marist College, as well as a Six Sigma Green Belt from Villanova University. She is also a longtime certified Reiki master, holds a degree in nutrition and wellness coaching from the Institute of Integrative Nutrition, and is a certified Yoga instructor.

Today, Kerr coaches people to start living their best unicorn lives. She lives in the greater New York City area with her husband, Rob, their son, Ryan, as well as her mom, sister, three dogs, and a cat.

She can be reached at info@boostlifecoach.com.

Are you ready to start living your most magical unicorn life? Boost® Life Coaching can take your magic spark and turn it into an incredible inferno that burns away doubt and leaves you with the life you've always dreamed of having. Val offers:

- One-on-one coaching to help make your biggest dreams a reality
- Small-group settings for support—and a safety net of connection
- Hands-on workshops to start putting your goals, dreams, and magical life into action
- Free resources to learn more about visioning, wellness, and unicorn life
- A community of people committed to living their best lives—and who want you to be part of their unicorn herd!

For more information,
visit www.BoostLifeCoach.com
or email Val at info@boostlifecoach.com.

www.ingramcontent.com/pod-product-compliance
Lightning Source LLC
LaVergne TN
LVHW051509070426
835507LV00022B/3019